Turning Mountain
Paul Wilson

Turning Mountain
Paul Wilson

I know where the god is hiding,
starved. I have slept
in the turning mountain.

John Newlove

WOLSAK
&WYNN

Cover art: Dorothy Knowles, *Dense Woods*, used with the permission of the artist and The Mackenzie Art Gallery, Regina
Cover design: Rachel Rosen
Typeset in Adobe Garamond, printed in Canada by The Coach House Printing Company, Toronto, Ontario

The publishers gratefully acknowledge the support of the Canada Council for the Arts and the Ontario Arts Council for their financial assistance.

Wolsak and Wynn Publishers Ltd
69 Hughson Street North, Ste. 102
Hamilton, ON
Canada L8R 1G5

National Library of Canada Cataloguing in Publication Data

Wilson, Paul, 1954-
    Turning mountain / Paul Wilson.

Poems.
ISBN 978-1-894987-19-6

    I. Title.

PS8595.I5844T87 2007   C811'.54   C2007-904995-8

*This book is for my mother, Gladys Davenport
and dedicated to the memory of Anne Szumigalski*

Landscape Theory

Field
Trips

Urge

A man wakes an hour before dawn.
He wanders through the house in darkness
as if he needs to reassemble his life.

He stops before a window and looks out at the apple tree,
its edges chewed by the night, a dark mass, a cold moon
that took to earth while he slept.

Soon he will place a ladder in the tree and climb into the calm
of the morning. He will be reminded of blossoms, white blossoms
brilliant in the rain as he reaches, cradles three apples in each palm.

For twelve years he has risen early to harvest the tree, before birds,
before wasps, before apples turn soft as tongues, and reek
with their own vinegar. He is awake now, beckoned by an urge
he must surrender to.

He stands at the window learning again the rhythm that has brought
him to this moment. He reasons with the slower heart. He senses
lightness in his hands when apples appear, red whorls of light
in the burdened branches of the tree.

The bountiful eye

The snapdragon holds me with its petals,
deep as blood, the whole summer pulsing.

The zucchini swallows an underground river – from rhizome,
through vine, I sense a flow to white seeds at the core of the flesh.

There is an end to beans, salvaged for one meal
to steam then quick fry with butter and slivered almonds.

Among the raspberries you cut. Dead canes lean
on the new growth. You wear gloves against the dry nettles.

I imagine us returning here after years away. The garden
cared for by a slothful tenant – our memories overgrown,

perennials choked by weeds, dill jangling the air.
We sit among the tangle without a thought of spades or shears.

In this most joyful of gardens we turn from neglect
and rest our weary bodies on a bed of yarrow.

We spend a warm afternoon disrupting
the chaos, part spindly stalks to find knots of herbs.

We are intent on the simple seed, seek in the garden
the signature of loss, our many small and bountiful deaths.

The irises

In reply to the question:
What can I do? Your irises
bloom again after two years.

This zeal the iris has
for the moment: purple petals,
white beard rocking in the breeze.

I am a fool for meaning, yet I think
of Wittgenstein's Oriental carpet.
The one he dreamt, and was haunted by.

Its pattern was always the same –
leaf, petal, entry, no entry;
the traps of seeing, not seeing.

Still this morning I gazed upon irises
and perhaps they gazed back. I cut them
and brought them to your room.

Now ask me how many lives have the irises?
Ask for us, how many? After love:
love again.

Between the orchard and the sky

My daughter and I meet a blind magpie
on the path to the orchard.
His dark head cocks toward the call of a high flyer.
We stand looking down, his cloudy eyes roll back
in his head as if in a dream of three desires –
the egg, the sky and the wings of the sun.

The bird's beak opens, tongue curling, soundless.
My daughter would touch its iridescent tail, peer into opaque eyes.
She grips my hand when the bird's neck strains skyward.
Tail feathers ruffle and without a cry the magpie's wings flitter.
Suddenly tail, white wings divide light as the bird flies,
a faltering pulse as it strikes into the woods.

The magpie wings break through underbrush
until we hear a rest, a deeper silence.
I turn to my child, and tell her we cannot follow
for I see she would if I let go. I lift her onto my shoulders
and walk towards the clearing. She looks back,
not ahead to the orchard.

My daughter has found the sweetest plum,
and claims there is *a God behind God.* Looking up into the
laden branches she slurps fruit through purple skin and I tell her:
Your God made birds first, but they were blind and roosted
in his long beard and on his broad shoulders, afraid to fly.
God made floating trees, in a watery world.
The birds smelt blossoms and flew inside God's trees to sleep.

Each bird tucked its head under a wing and saw mountains
and meadows of many worlds. They woke with vision
and with a longing for distance that pulsed in their wings.

My daughter spits a slippery pit into her palm
and tosses it from the shadow of the plum tree
into the fierce midday light. We do not see it land.

Field trips

Twenty children, eight parents, and one teacher – he takes
rear duty on the valley path. *Everything lives* says his daughter
who points to goldenrod, a round gall on its stem. *Something
lives in here*, she says taping the hard gall. He shows her
hawthorn bushes. She measures her pinkie against the longest
thorn, and imagines a claw of thorns.

*To go down into water, he wants to go after the teacher, to dive
after the two boys who were sucked into the lake when the sandbar
collapsed. The white arm to shore gone. He shuffles his feet, the boys
cluster, holding hands in silence.*

He carries his daughter over an abandoned beaver dam, she closes
her eyes. He tells her the dam is stronger than the brick house
of the three pigs, because beavers build their houses to dance on in
the moonlight when no one is watching. Their houses stand solid
as they pirouette, jump and fan their flat tails in the milky light.
They dance because nothing is stronger than mud and sticks.

*He stands on the sand with the other boys, stares inside the
blackness of the water, sees holes there, holes he needs to fill
and fill again. The teacher begs them to move before more
of the sandbar collapses. They will not walk to the island now.
Wet and exhausted the teacher kneels on the sand, hands over
his face. There must be a cave below the island, simple shelter
where otters sleep, where the boys would be warm. He thinks
this but he cannot speak to the teacher or the others. The wind
blows stronger off the island, the boys around him begin to whimper.*

When the path loops back to the creek, banks are overrun,
the rock bridge is washed out. Laughing, he and the other
adults wade into the creek, form a chain, a bridge of arms
to lift the children and pass them one by one over the water.
The children gather at the other bank, watch the effort of their
mothers, fathers as each child is lifted above the water,
cradled for an instant and passed on. They call out the names
of their friends and cheer their arrival on shore.

He imagines the silence before the helicopter came. He
had turned to the island, and was watching the birds as
they trolled above the water then dove below the surface.
Hum below his feet as if the children were speaking, making
sounds at the backs of their mouths *rak, rak, rak*. He sensed
they were pointing, fingers for weapons *dead, dead, you're
dead* they chanted below the water. He looked up, a man
lowered on a rope was holding his arms out over the water.
In the echo of a voice, from the white walls of his secret
cave he heard the man call his own name.

Opening the cottage

Opening the cottage we step into a deep breath of winter
held from the sun. Yet there is something in these rooms
that is known to the ear – words from a folk tale. Someone
lost in a green forest, hears the clean chop of the woodsman.

We have emigrated from another season
where each morning we awoke within a hard, white fist.
We had only our breaths and our warm skin to coax
the slow hand of daylight.

It comes back to us, this little season made common
by the sun. Our bones want the welter of hammock days.
We listen for a story read near a glowing window,
words rising toward the prospect of kin.

We imagine perpetual summer, but know better.
We must wait to float on the cool, forgiving lake.
We must force ourselves to remember the colour of trees.
A door is flung open, and we drink warm air.

Underturn

All day wind funnels down the valley. I stand up
on God's Hill, hear whispers in the face of the wind, murmurs
my body throws off – the staccato beat of my shirt collar.

The trees below me are ecstatic in the light
their boughs hasten to meet the wind, bend
then snap up, then sway.

This ordered perception is a way of being false; I am like the wind
that would have us believe the world has not changed.
I am not alone; the bright fluke of the lake churns with whitecaps.

This morning my daughter asked, *Dad, about this God no God thing?*
At twelve she reads theology for what she doesn't know –
a way to touch the dance of grasses. In the church-camp below,

children volley words *There ain't no flies on us* I plant my feet
on dry soil and gather voices. All day from the northwest the wind
leans into the lake, the wind reaches deep – an underturn by evening.

Cold water from the depths is drawn upward and tonight
under a wide-mouth moon I will wade into the bone-chill shallows,
the wind will be calm and the dark hills will tremble
on the surface of the water.

The atmosphere that surrounds the body

Already the sun heats the sand so that it burns the soles of my feet.
The boys do not sound the cold as they stride into the lake,
water to their ankles, to their calves, to their thighs. Their skin
speaks to them of the climbing sun, and of night's retreat into water.

When I call them, when they turn and see the camera, they stand
stiff as crossing guards, as if they had just stepped into a second world.
The light transforms the cutbanks behind them into golden pyramids.
The boys look to shore, their voices lost.

Water reflects the gold hills but their bodies
point to land, thin reflections on the dark water. Hands
at their sides, just below the surface. Their gaze,
turned inward, as if deafly, dumbly they invent the lake.

I do not know what calls attention to the body in this place
where water and land have become mutable. The atmosphere
that surrounds the body is explicit in the fierce light. I am stopped
by a plurality of seeing what is imagined or lost before the lens opens.

I put the camera down, wave to the boys. They become arched arms,
buoyant bodies that dive and emerge, closer to the sun. The wind
shifts, and suddenly cools my skin. My hands reach for shadow,
and I think of the dark underbelly of lake ice in winter.

I turn my back to a palm of fire, relentless
in its rise through a cloudless sky.

Reading Tu Fu in a hammock, Last Mountain Lake

Above me dragonflies troll,
jagged in their hunt for prey.
One lands on my chest,
its saw-tooth jaws moving
up and down
as if speaking
of lifespan – of joy.

On the beach below a small child cries,
Papa, Papa, stay,
I imagine water and light
a halo around his body as he sinks
beneath a green wave.

Pelican on a tree-top current
casts a shadow that is the length of a tall man.
I look up – black wing tips are motionless.
Suddenly I too am travelling, my arms sensing
verbs of the wing. I sense a wider span
yet I am held here,
suspended in a hammock
woven from silence.

Recipe for sugaring the luna moth

A bottle of stale beer, cup of brown sugar,
dollop of molasses, plunk of rum, one rotten
banana (mashed). Let mixture sit for a week in the shade.

Timing is important, paint the spirits onto tree bark
precisely at twilight and wait until the night becomes
rich with wings. Return to your sugaring by candlelight.

You will find many moths, the white underwing,
the robin moth, with half moons on its wings,
but you've waited for the luna moth, the one come back
from the deep past, its green wings dusted
with random thoughts of the dead.

It will stay with you, drinking its fill,
but do not touch those trembling wings.
If the luna were not inebriated, if he were not dreaming
of a cool white flame, the moth might whisper to you:

*Do not worry the dead hear you, the light and the shambles
of your prayers, they hear it all. In summer afternoons they see
the heat, touch your temple, the sudden falling into a dream
of a green moth, fluttering near a doorway,
speaking softly of final things.*

Spider dance

Sarah dreams it over again
in the top bunk. She whispers her fears
to the small ones. Wakes as if dreaming
eyes fixed on knots in the pine grain.
Here a face emerges from wood: it's Mr Toby
who bites off toes and fingers with his pike-mouth.
She has seen the hulking fish in green water
where the minnows skim, and slice into shadows –
and teeth shining.

She scans the ceiling corners for spiders
and tries not to think of her sister's claim:
Before we die each of us will swallow as many
as eight spiders. She sees one near the peak
legs crossed into four neat x's.

The spider knows air
the way Sarah knows dragonflies, their thin blue weaving
among sweet clover. The spider knows darkness
and the music of sleep the way Sarah knows lake bottom silt
and leeches that cling to toes, heels, and calves.
Somehow, her body is not repulsed by this knowing.

As dawn enters the cottage she remembers crouching
on the beach where wind had flattened lake grass
into a web on the sand.

She conjures up the one who rides the string over her breath,
makes no sound when it is sucked into the damp cave of her mouth,
when the teeth grind down. Even Mr Toby will not hear the descent.
Slip, slip, slip ...

She remembers spinning the way a spider might dance.
Looking up into a blueness no mouth can swallow.
Her feet tracing sand as she turned to the south
hands, and arms wild, to touch one great thing, the only thing,
and then throwing herself into the air and coming full circle
to face south again.

24

Aubade, Last Mountain Lake

This morning I watch my neighbor fish alone in his canoe
The sun is warm again and claims the two of us
He owns the cottage that tops the hill
and most afternoons he plays Sinatra, standards
that enter my thoughts like regret
worn small and round Today he turns sixty
alone   his wife left him last Christmas
yet he will tell me that devotion is a serenade
the last swim of the season under a rising moon
and northern lights *Just sing along*   he says to anyone
who visits   his baritone slipping under Frank's tenor
lifting the song into golden leaves

This morning age is dispersed by the genius of light
He lifts then plunges his paddle   gliding to shore
I think of going to him   embracing this man   a celebration of two
Not even crows   raucous in the blazing poplars can diminish
the affluence of this moment   My wife and children are asleep
in the shuttered cottage while I wait in a world
among spent worlds   and know what it is we cannot hold

This evening I will pass the neighbor on the beach
and want to say   *nothing lasts*   but we will pass
in silence   we will both look south to a distant marsh
where countless birds sing for a journey they must take by night

Transport

He hands his daughter the binoculars, she peers
through them at the churning flock. There is no centre,
the plenitude of light on lake waves,
on the backs of snow geese. Here he thinks,
right here, he could fall to earth with them,
feel their thirst beneath the sky.

The geese lose focus in the light
and he feels a drowsiness, as if his very existence
were giving in, as if he were drinking up the warmth
around him for a journey inscribed within.
He closes his eyes and sees swirling white geese,
the clamor of their voices in his ears.

He is inside the flock, a floating instinct
that listens to their deep language. He raises his hands
to touch wing beat. Something breaks
into the sky. "Look," his daughter points. Geese rise
off the water, transforming into one silver body,
a mandala revolving.

He is stunned by their sudden burst into allegro.
He feels lighter, light working over wings as the skein
folds and unfolds. The trees, the lake – this is ragged seeing,
a moving out from opulence. The sky is tethered
and the birds move through, casting
a broken shadow, a presentiment.

His blood, his heart has not had its fill
of grass and of wind. He lifts his arms,
unable to draw himself closer to the birds,
or his own devotions. Then he sees his daughter
running toward the shore, arms held out. She is flying
in the transport of her joy.

Thanksgiving

Overnight the tree has given up its fevered leaves.

I see a branch, pale as bone.
Last spring I cut the limb above it, to bring air
and light into the tree. In this hour the spirit is helpless,
hidden in the blaze of these tumbled garments
blown down from a space in the sky.

I empty ice from buckets, cut hollyhocks from the garden.
Empty my pockets: stones I have carried, stones that carry
a scent of the sun. I empty my dreams
into morning, each image, each rag,
a possibility to be raised into the sky.

I prepare for a season that feeds on itself. I traverse
the frozen ground, from the trunk to the bounds of the tree's reach.
Here in the tree's shadow frost whitens the earth.
Soon everything distinct will be forfeited
and in the fields annihilation will swell with each bright hour.

Even as it climbs, as it comes back to the tree,
the sun in its depletion
wants nothing.

Forgiveness

The snow is falling and all the world's news drags
behind me like cordwood or reconciliation.
I see a light across the creek, a window where a man
and a woman sit at a table, too weary to speak of the day.
How long before words are spoken?

In their silence they shift their bodies more slowly than life:
he scratches an itch under his collar. Sewing a button
to work shirt, she snips the thread with her teeth.
What is needed, a lie, a prayer or both?

We always sense the earth in our bodies. Even frozen
we open it for one remembered, for one long forgotten.
Soon the man will take up the bones and play
his clattering hurt.

I will walk back to you, and I will speak or be stopped by exhaustion,
the way snow in its slow resistance stops everything.

Near midnight, in a silent room, with all I know of forgiveness.

Kiwi

I peel the thin skin of kiwi. Each winter morning
my daughter asks for the green tartness,
a simple desire that will evaporate soon enough.

Where is my devotion to her now? Is it like the disappearance
of snow: first powder, then crystalline skin, and finally —
a ghost on the lawn?

Ten years ago I carried her, through inconsolable hours,
whispered into her small ear, *this little while, a little while more.*

My daughter reads Yeats' folk tales
and sees me as fallen, a one-winged angel,
not good enough to be saved nor bad enough to be lost.

The small furry fruit feels warm, alive in my palms.
Each morning she reads me, her heart closed, she keeps her distance
from my disreputable breath. She asks, *What is a martyr,
and why are there so many in Ireland?*

She waits for an answer as if all restless things
could be saved by time. The kiwi's skin falls away in strips.
I halve it and offer the fruit to my daughter,
green juice in the lines of my hands.

She falls silent, sees in the speckled black seeds a small truth
I had forgotten about the vanishing night sky.

At the Woodrow Lloyd Memorial

Sunlight skims ghosts of snow. I shiver and think of Woodrow
Lloyd as a child skating on a frozen lake, always leaping ahead –
eleven years old, when he entered high school.

I clear snow from the face of the cairn. Ice fills the serif font
of Frost's brass stanzas. Woodrow Lloyd walked here, pausing
in the hollow hum of Albert Street traffic.

Under the elms and spruce did he think of Frost,
his paths, his roads, his mutable woods, and his winter hours?
Did Woodrow recall Swan Lake School, 1932?

How to nurture minds when stomachs are empty –
when hope is a poem, a prayer repeatable in darkness?
Woodrow is electric as he reads; the students hear the *sigh*

in his voice, a deepening sorrow in the words.
Woodrow senses them listening as never before. The wind
gnaws at the sills, door jams, dirt clacks against window panes.

In this classroom no one will fail to choose, no one will fall.
Woodrow holds up a photograph of Frost slouched, rumpled
in a coat and tie. It is a face a farm boy might recognize as fatherly,

weary eyes, barely open. Each student holds the image,
and is drawn by Frost's gaze to the long bones of his hand,
to the sharp nib poised above the blank page.

Here at the Memorial, where the path divides,
I imagine Woodrow standing utterly still. Not speech,
but language in his head– *Though as for that the passing there …*

As he walks the wooded path, then the four slow blocks to his home,
he wonders if it is something that came to him in sleep,
this unswerving self, somehow unalterably lost to its opposite.

Even to rhythm and the caressing of an idea there is no solution.
I stand *bent in the undergrowth,* and dream Woodrow here,
half-sheltered from the wind, meditating on
the persistence of metaphor.

The
Crows

The regret of dreams

The dead insist on dreams of idleness.
They slump in a chair I inherited,
intently thrumming moon-white fingernails
on Spanish leather and speaking scant words
about their last garden, their first lover.
That room I return to with sunflowers
leaning out from wallpaper. A phone rings
and the sunflowers turn their gentle heads.

Ear to the wall I recollect this voice,
one that listens, that plunders my first home
where my spine unfurled like a frond,
where villages of moths whirred the lamps
golden – where my eyes shut for everyone,
a burnt seed clutched in my sleeping hand.

Man sleeping

A man reclines on a sofa, model for his wife who has painted him in
this pose over twenty years. Her hand, her brush, has followed this
unfolding on the few nights he cannot bring himself to paint. In his
hands he holds a photograph, an orange and a ball of cut glass. His feet
are crossed, left over right as always. He holds the ball of buttery light
and watches colours splash over his shirt.

There is a persistent needling in her head; he has changed so much, yet
you must have this sameness. As she paints he ponders the photograph,
the day it was taken. The two of them stand in a frame of ancient
columns. There is the rasping of cicadas, fierce sun. She is ill and sleeps
in the shade of a ruin. Cats wind and unwind the grass, their mewing
sounds in the heat. She made a sound too, a fever drone low at first
then rising in her throat. He brings her water, a kerchief, cool and wet.
As he thinks of these things he drifts off to sleep.

The glass ball rolls from his hand and across the floor to where she
stands. The sound of his breathing is the sound of her brush, she thinks.
She looks at the painting and decides it is good. She smells the crisp
fragrance of orange. He must have broken the peel with a fingernail.
She puts the brush down and picks up the glass, heavy in her hand,
unchanged all these years. She lays a blanket over him then covers her
canvas. She places the orange, the photograph and glass ball at the foot
of the sofa, near his shoes. When does one begin thinking with the
heart, she asks, how long before one stops? He will wake in the dark,
she thinks, and turns off the light.

The hat

In this portrait the hat glows.
Illusion exposes luck, thinks the man from China.
Wearing it he is weightless in a new world.
The hat lights his way
through a thousand valley nights
until he finds his land tilled and wet,
shallow waves in the sun. He will tell you
the hat is woven from strands of golden silk,
the maker whispered dragon songs
into the bowl, a wish for every free man.
He cannot bear to part with a hat lit from within
by his own vanishing future.

The hat looks out from the photograph
and wants to fly into the glossy finish of this century,
to adorn the heads of CEOs.
It would bring the unknown man along
for the ride, someone to stand on tiptoe
and place the haloed hat on graying heads,
his face resolute, his eyes set on the colours
of their neckties. The man smiles
when fiscal giants place manicured hands
on his thin shoulders. He nods
as they admire their brilliant faces
in a mirror his mother brought from China.

The hat in this photograph wants to wear time down,
to show its small power, a beguiling diversion at the G-8 summit,
seen on the heads of the heads of state. The hat
wants to live now and forever in the minute implosions
of a thousand cameras.

Figure

How long before I live only in the memories
of the ones I've forgotten? To pass through
their thoughts as image: man, child, or ancient –
naked, thin or bent. Where hollow awareness begins,
there is a large fieldstone to stand on,
voices from the sky.

After a long day there is sunlight
on skin, a book spine stands out
from across the room, the title
burned off. This is habitation
of the instant, a light where I have no place,
no voice.

A brief incarnation, I float
beyond the reflection in a picture window,
a face remembered, half in shadow
clutched to my chest – a book,
a bunch of daffodils, or the tallest weeds
in the garden.

I turn, a shape in the mind, eyes open.
The forgotten ones snare me. *There you are,*
they murmur. I am on my way to them,
with strangeness and the raw accumulation
of being. I will arrive, a sleeping man,
armed by sleep.

On the fieldstone is a book, inside
is a drawing of the delicate muscles
of the inner ear, rip out the page
and hear the voice of a child
who says over and over *when I was here,*
when I was here before.

What would I give to remember
that final time? When all perception is lost.
When form splinters, and memory breaks
in the sun. When I am unsocketed
in the mind, of the one forgotten,
the one reborn.

Making it dark

In the bookstore today, a woman
with the alphabet tattooed down the length
of her spine. Imagine her lover whispering:
Lets do it while singing just the letters,
a quatrain here between my forefinger
and thumb. Lets turn out the lights and sing
a little death.

Up late I think of the hypothermic climber
lost in a mountain crevasse. Lips blue
he recites colours: red beret, green valise,
pink eraser, yellow pencil.
He cannot see the helicopter that circles
and circles the empty mountain.
The climber cannot imagine the oleander
blooming in my dark living room. Unseen
the flowers smell of their whiteness

It is true that all we want from words
are the shadows that they bring us.
The breath heavy, the font bold
as we read the last words we will
ever read. Our lips move as we say
the words silently, say them aloud.
On our tongues they become salt,
a taste we must tell again,
in the language of light.

The missing dolls

He bolts upright in bed, he senses they are sighing
from another place, his *naked babies.*

He called them *naked* until his wife dressed them as dolls.
He is filled with a vision: the shop door is thrown open, glass
on the floor, every baby, gone. A ripping burn pins his arm;
each breath draws a splintered peg from his lungs.

He always made two by lunch, perched on his workbench,
staring out from the shade of ivy, the shadow of lace,
from the dark of sparrow grass. On each face he painted
two perfect black pupils, one to fade to blindness and one
to dream of willful murder.

Fingers curled inside each clay head, he murmured into ears
neat as shells, *There's never a man that makes such babies –
I make you with mouth red as rose death, eyes black
as the ruin of secrets.*

He would go down to the shop but his legs are heavy –
his body submerged. *Where then?* He says, as if expecting
an account from a ghostly witness. The heave and draw
of waves fills his ears. Pain rises in him
as dense as heartwood.

He slaps a fist to his chest, to his blood bellows, to his old storm.
Thousands of petal red lips fall open before his eyes. He looks
at his hands, good hands, clay marking each line. He sees
his hands fly from his body, blind and deaf to the stifled heart.

His hands soar over rooftops, their palms curled as if listening
for voices. The hands flex into warmth like clay touched
by the mind of God.

Memory from my future life

I sit in a chair in a stone room, write in the journal
on my lap. I sit for hours, watch shadows cross the walls,
the floor, write down thoughts. That scent from the garden
and the metal hum of insects clear and sharp.
                                            To forget is natural,
what I don't remember, all natural as breath.

The chair remembers it was built in an another century
from the rough planks of a gun box. The table
reinvests itself, the sun's last light revealing gouges,
scratches that my fingers trace and retrace. I light a candle,
gather food: half a meat pie, three over-ripe avocados
and three opened wine bottles, all red.

A guest arrives. I had this written down. I embrace him
with what seems to be dignity. We eat. He talks. I look
into his face, the kind of face in which one could confide one's
first true lines. Finally, silence.

I tell him, *Nothing is lost to forgetting.*
He clasps my soft hands and smiles with what might
be his idea of dignity. I draw back, propose a toast:

To memory as a station where we all disembarked
in our father's arms, the platform wide with light.
To the station gone now to fire or dust,
and to the train's howl,
distant and soft as a whispered lie.

We raise our glasses and see they are empty.

Dusk

The shadow rises, a moth-blue belt in the east,
a dusty hoop ascending through a cloudless sky,
earth's ghostly shadow hunching toward night.

You said once, *When you die you will be the water*
still warm, that drains from the tub.
The water that sounds like a small voice
singing backwards, you said,
if you are first to die.

Wheeling overhead a moth, gray irises on its wings,
lights on my wrist. I touch a wing and the moth flies
in and out of light. Dusk is broken by the descent
of bats. Suddenly, a memory of you by the window,
the shadow of the earth reflected over
your left shoulder, your eyes closed.
I watched you through dusk, unable to enter
your water dreams, moths gathering – over your head
their soft bodies shuddering against the pane.
Here it is again tonight, this sad arousal I cannot elude.
I will be water, I will be moth, I will be in the tongue of the moth,
awakening an ancient thirst for fire.

Words fall

His hands are much older than the rest of him.
Cupped hands that reach to enfold unformed things:
the white smoke of burning weeds, the blue shadow
of a magpie's tail. Words wait at the peppery edge of light.

He names what can be named. Trees blossom in the buzz
of spring: *plum, peach, pear.* In his body – water,
air, ancestors, vice – all these things he took in and wrote
into his poems. His hands turn over the night's first stars.

With this seeing he marked time, rotated mulch. Words
infiltrated his hands, instilled bone-joints, and muscle with
lucidity. Words fell from his hands as bitten nails, dead skin.
Beneath snow his astonishment was at rest – poetry receded.

Tonight, with a wooden hoe he turns earth over word.
The mossy sigh of the silt reminds him of what he left untold.
On his knees he is birthless, deathless. His hands dig
in the speckled soil, his face lifts to the night.

Raindrops fall to earth. They fill his eyes
and he shivers with the joy of unseeing.

All Souls'

The night you died I imagined you on a Cornwall beach
your slip held high, salt foam rising to your thighs.

The fish flashed gold between your plump feet, and I thought
it must be the hardest thing about death, that first night.

Getting used to it all – light, soul being and death itself –
which you always said was such a small part of things.

When All Souls' came I lit candles in a rotted-out stump
and placed there the skull of a greyhound that had outrun

his master and was ripped apart by coyotes.
Had you been here we might have spoken of the female,

how she stood outside the pack stepping up in silence,
tearing flesh from the mauled carcass.

Whose voice was it, mulling over the words: *she cradles blood
in her mouth, and later her pups drink
at her heavy tongue, rip meat from her jaws.*

At 35, after giving birth, blood haemorrhaged
from your body and death appeared in your doctor's eyes.

Yet this was death diminished,
when set against life with your children. Not yet –
better get on with it. Go away, surgeon, you say

I will light candles in the grandmother tree.
I will count the orbits of the moon,

the tiny white tablets dissolved in my blood, and the fish
in my poems. I will write these things into an equation, you say.

That first flickering night in the afterworld I will sing
along the way and swim among the bruised reeds

quickening the fish in their vast salt-water grave.

The Crows

1. *Scarecrow*

Someone has left a pomegranate propped against the fieldstone
that is your marker. A red leathery heart lost on the green; crows
have ripped at the sapphire seeds, a darker flesh in their throats.
Three crows sit in a tree, like poet thugs, and have much to say
about the nest of your bones. Between their gurgling praise they
snip leaves with their beaks, green leaves fall at my feet, at the foot
of your grave. It's as if the crows say, "Make wings of your life move
wider than the mind in steely starlight, highwire a storm, take it
further into the day."

I don't know, is a beginning. You taught me never settle for a
choice of two possible worlds, you said, go deeper, call back
the wilderness of the dreamt child. The child made of cork who
bobbed, and bobbed on the surface of the world running through
aspen stands and building grass towers in his mind. Say it again
before nightfall, *I don't know where?* Then ask the crows to take me.
They chortle between themselves as if wondering at my presence
here when you left long ago for the underworld. Even the sudden
wind wants a departure lifting the waxy leaves from my feet,
pushing over the pomegranate. The hunger beads are scattered
on the ground, a haphazard atonement, not meant for you but for
the living who travel here to stand below the torment of crows.

I cast back to a time when I knew you were writing and I imagine
shadows of trees climb the silence of your yard, the beehive dance
of your voice revives seasons, your *tum, tum, tumble* of words, and you
afloat in a broken sea. Your voice rouses the fish in their pond who
swish jeweled tails and rise to kiss the wide dome of the sky.

2. *A slow remembering of the dead*

I awoke with restraint in my arms, and legs
but in my hands the burn of intention.
I stepped softly into the still dark
and could smell danger before I saw the sleeping crows.
They roosting above, below my door and the scent
of old clothes and the remnants of dead hair
rose out of the earth, up through my dew wet feet.
Bluesy, and shaking I stood among the crows
as if to relinquish the memory of many burials
and much weeping. Nothing to do but bloody sing:

Bone broke, crow throat
Who is it that I call?
Eye gone, crow yawn
Who is it after all?

I sang among the waking crows.

3. *The underworld*

The landscape springs open from her life: Bad Lands, the Big Muddy, a
vast dry land. Nearby a wasp's nest under the hummed earth, hoodoos
rise, hiss in the heat. She walked this land, and I with crows at my
shoulder walk toward a hole, night ground, below a weakened sun. I
look down and the crows flap then fly into me and I fall. Soundless
wings flutter near my face, I taste carrion breath. There are no angels,
no light. Dark wings set me down, and the crows fall away as if flying
through earth.

I find her as one is enfolded by a garden at night. She is before me,
behind me, larger and lesser than when I last saw her. There is water
running nearby, my eyes make out watery clouds reflected on stone
walls. She speaks as if I had just returned with the tea, "Speed is a
common complaint here, the speed of hands and feet, how they are
in constant motion, a blur, temporal as hummingbird's wings to
the human eye. Yet, this lift, this flight is good, great, almost like

swimming. Here they flit around muttering, 'My hands, my feet, where are they taking me?' I say what's the point of transfiguration if you're always moaning about the logic of flesh. Take that poet over there, the gangly one who claims to have once had hands the size of Newfoundland. It's sad how he can't draft a word without his mortal hands to guide him."

I ask her to still herself, and to come back to the world. Come back, I say and sing again. Old soul, old flame, no one can cock an ear to the wasp's papery song like you. Come back swift or slow, come back to the hoary vowels of earth. She disappears, I am aware of stones moving into shadow. Then her voice thin, striding ahead of me: "Oh beware," she says, "beware of what you ask of the dead. Never leave one world with a desire for another … go back and stand in your garden at the end of summer and think of a shape that moves you.

Take hold of branches, and let your weight bend them and let them hold your grief. Stare up at the grey worsted sky and plant three saplings while you wait for rain." With a clattering of stones her presence is gone.

I open my eyes and find myself standing on a grid road at dusk. A thread of black in the sky, crows winging into invisibility. A wind, perhaps from the lungs of the dead, pushes hard at my shoulder, with all that I have left behind I listen: *There is no road and no direction.*

Swept

The body's belief in death is simple, true, taken up
by the unwilled muscle that fills then empties the lungs –
this comes to him as he walks to the apple tree.

Even in sleep he sighed: *oh so little,* then snorted:
more is not enough. Now, he buries his face in apple blossoms,
a slow assured breath, the scent surrounding him in silk.

Last night he tried to drink the past into submission,
he itemized lost cargo on a dark sea. Yet his body insisted on sleep,
dreamless depths where body and death are one illusion.

He wrote a list when drunk, his memory a cellar
of homemade wines: *plum, rosehip, dandelion, apple.*
The pencil ripped a line between *sweet red* and *dry crab.*

There is a ladder in the tree and he climbs it.
Overhead bees persistently build tiny snowballs of pollen.
He feels their vibrations in the vein down the centre of his tongue.

A dry leaf he thinks, his tongue curling on the roof of his mouth.
He imagines wind, a storm to sweep away these blossoms. He hears
the movement of the tree, as music, as disposition.

He licks his lips to taste the world, as if flesh
were fruit, as if in this moment he were the flaw
within the blossom.

A morning in December

This morning frost etches every elm branch white.
Here black rooftops, crowned trees are carved
by a hard-edged light. Wind jostles the trees;
soon this blazing form will slip
from their stark branches.

I am not young. I prefer silence
to my simple poems. In transgression,
in prayer, morning and evening I ask
why stall?

How to surrender? Frost releases
in the wind. Tell me, what is it
that must be read aloud
and where is the small god who listens?

The Empress & the peonies

We want to know what the peonies know
about the sun, for they live if undisturbed root
to petal for a hundred years. We want to know
what peonies know about pain, to be still
and unyielding as if the earth with its many mouths
was never false.

There was a time when flowers could hear
spirits and the songs of the Empress.
To her, seeds were thoughts and her garden flesh
she could make bloom, or blush with a whispered command.
One spring morning she ordered all her flowers to open
precisely at dawn.

Their opening would be a deeper seeing, her heart
scattered over ten thousand fluttering petals. Yet the peonies
remained closed. Though she drew a blade
in anger the Empress could not cut the peonies down. And so
they lived long after she had died and the palace
garden had been overrun by ragweed.

Before we become unseeing, unhearing, we want
to know what the peonies know about death. Here dried
and hung on the wall, there is no flaunt in them, no fragrance.
The nectary parched, crumbles under the touch. We want to
know this century-deep loss. O peonies
let this time we have be a dying into being.

On a cloud I saw a child*

I was broke when they asked me to carve the baby, so I said
yes. Portland stone is pure and old, a hundred million years of
gray resistance. Hit it with a chisel, it goes "dink". You can't bully
it, but if you're humble, if you're patient, you can carve it.

I'm not a churchgoer but sitting on that block of stone, I prayed.
I read Blake for vision, drank scotch for inspiration. Then it came
to me, like raw will. I stood and swept the rulers and compasses
right off the block and I started to carve, heard myself calling,
"We'll get you out, we'll get you out of here soon!"

Portland stone has a sweet, pungent smell. Quarrymen say it
has healing powers, safe to rub into a cut– but they are great
liars. Yet something is healed in me. To remove a ton of stone
to get down to a baby's leg, an arm, an ear. Stone comes alive
when you make it vulnerable. A nun came into my workshop
then shushed me while she prayed. I stood head bowed, silent,
until she left.

The child sinks into the pocked stone as if a cloud held him up.
One leg is bent, lifted in the air, delicate and plump. His fingers
are curled into tiny fists, one at his open mouth. The umbilical
cord was the last thing to appear. It winds its way under his leg
and back into the stone. That part is my joy.

They've placed him in Trafalgar Square, a stone Christ for the
Christmas crib. I'm having trouble letting go. The stillness of his
body gone, the heavy untamed stillness. I have this vision of me
on a camp bed, each night guarding him, guarding the stone. Yet
all this time I know it's been the other way around.

*from *Songs of Innocence*, William Blake

On a poem titled "Beloved"

How far a poem wanders from the regime
of the book. Turn to its page and the poem is gone.
Imagine an afterlife, the poem locked in the mind
of a travelling monk, its measure and marking
placed on a makeshift shrine, near a smiling Buddha.

The poem was written in a long spell between poems.
On a train in the night it woke saying, *Did you hear that?*
The poem understands destinations, roads, untracked earth.
The poem has found a man who is looking for treasure,
religious relics buried in the Gobi by his grandfather.

The poem loves the disordered grace of the man's memory,
how his eye picks out one stone among a million stones
and knows what lies beneath. The poem enters his mind
the way an eye can touch land. The poem gives emptiness
a path, a footprint and a face.

Digging does not end until dark when the man sleeps. The poem
slips into his palm, weaving itself among his fingers feeling
in the dark for a word: *lost;* a word: *splendour.* Don't ask why
things close the way they do.

The man stirs, turns closer to the treasure,
in his hand, the poem pleads: *Do not go back to sleep!*

Landscape
Theory

The release

(May 17, 2004, Old Man on His Back, Saskatchewan)
for Sharon & Peter Butala

We have no measure for their vanishing.

I listen in four directions though I can't remember dreaming
sky, and earth. Say it humbly, *the bison have returned.*

We stand behind straw-bale blinds our eyes follow lines
we have no story for. The bison crest the ridge,
uncertain at the gate.

Fifty yearlings, ragged in their winter coats, they balk,
heads swinging. The riders close behind, their horses step
muscles straining to the south. Just north of here men once shot
bison from rail cars. So many they barely had to aim, brandy
and cigar at hand, and the gentlemen felled
the bison at the speed of steel.

A scruffy heifer passes through, then breaks, the herd follows,
running the fence-line before wheeling around to pass before us.
Their fierce hooves praise the earth; this thunder turns
into north-wind and from their throats comes a kind of weeping,
the thrust of a long singing once heard but not understood.

Now the bison walk above and below the stars
and the lichen and the grass and the rain and the stones

and all is returned to them and returned again.

Horse Theatre

(After a mural by Bob Boyer)

Horse theatre rides toward us from a time
before fences, before ropes. These four horses remember
short grass days, eating wheatgrass, buffalo grass.
They remember a time before humans blinded horses
into wagon-trail seeing. A time when all eternity
lay open for pleasing the ghost horses of the wind.

See their colours at dawn:
silt, fire, snow, sun.

Horse theatre depends on two times – the hour of the run
when horses sail the plains, the way cloud horses sail the sky;
and the hour of drama when storm and lightning split
horse-spirit into fear and theory. West of time, they eat,
and sleep with the earth. In the dry season they drink from
The Creek Before Where the Bones Lie.

See their colours at midday:
clay, sky, cloud, smudge.

The horses may believe they are audience. Perhaps they almost
exist here, where long ago stood a few willow and cherry bushes,
but no wood for fuel. Perhaps they look out at our urban order,
with a sense of the pantomime. Yet there is no servitude
in their eyes. The four horses ride on with measured endurance;
they ride on, triumphant.

See their colours at nightfall:
sand, rain, creek, moon.

Landscape theory

1.

Here artists rarely lose sight
of landscape. Here they paint
a pure sky, an immense seeing
that rotates around a small black point
no light can penetrate.

This point of darkness is at the centre
of a yellow canola field, near
the blind choices of a fallen
farmer, not far from a slough that later
reflects a night sky smeared with stars.

This point might inhabit
the parkland meadow of a Knowles,
the boreal lake of a Lindner.
Look closely, though barely visible
you sense the point's vulnerability
below the vast sky,
salient, yet insignificant.
Small, still, yet breathing.

2.

Drive here at night and be moved, or not.
See each farm, each dwelling lit up –
human constellation, or monument
to will? Hear the growl of dogs,
when the rains come, when the rains come
too late. Once more everything exists,
every possibility for salvage.

This is not a land of lament; we do not allow it.
This is not a land where ecstatic poets
read stories to the dead.
Yet, often we look to the sky
and read the flesh of fable in clouds.

Grandfathers wait in stations, sleep in stations
dream the land enters the room, scratchgrass on skin.
They wake, feed the fire, go off into the blue, into the mud,
and in the dry season they stand on dust, herd the crop.
Grandmothers find within themselves eyes, hands,
feet, the rough outline of a human life. They watch
life walk the land in unmeasured time.

Only form remains, to inhabit.
In each prairie city light obliterates the stars.
Light fills all the rooms, we hear geese overhead
and we say, this is our domain.

The past is a theory hardly a soul remembers.
Pain doesn't make us live. Intent doesn't make us safe.

When seeing fails

The head of night rests on the mountain – my mind
shuffles into its own blindness. My seeing curves, like a rush
of dark water. My hands, my voice reel out a prayer for a fish
with scales the colour of honey.

The night scope, its infrared light, finds the deer's breast,
alive as the hunter's eye relaxes, his lungs take in air – dead
before he exhales. The deer topples; its darkening body
a metaphor to rest the eyes on.

Smoke is a red veil for the moon. I think of all that can go wrong
with seeing. A blotch of color, now a white tail in deep grass, a stone
pulsing, slick with blood. There is a sequence the eye craves
as if death can never be trapped.

I think my way around a prone body, dream a scenario about one
who survives her own death, a red moon glimpsed through
a dim lens. There is always deflection, the eye shaded, even at night
these brief moments when I see just what it is I must not see.

Saltbush

The bird in the saltbush will not show itself but it cries:
the cry of hunger or the cry that swallows hunger? The bird
will not fly though I rattle the bush, peer into the thick tangle,

its song sung loud, insistent, a code shot from a liquid lung.
It is dry and cattle have grazed on the heavy green leaves.
I lick the underside of a leaf and taste alkali.

There is a story of a child, who was lost for days in these hills.
Nearly starved he was found in a clump of saltbush hiding
from searchers, strangers. The child had covered his face

with leaves and when he finally spoke, a gagged word fell
from his pale green tongue to the earth. When he spoke again,
it was names, many names that had not been heard

in this place before, and as he stood
birds flew up and cattle waded into shallow water.

Notes for touring the Museum of Winter

Walk barefoot over cold linoleum,
feel a chill rise in your bones. Read words
of hope, words of devotion for another year's
yield written on a dusty old calendar.

In this kitchen kernels rattle in a tin cup
on a red table cloth. In all the windows,
a cloudless night. Go out and huddle
with the cattle turn your back to the north wind.

Just crossing the fields can kill you.
You feel a dependence that comes from living
in the dark. You keep the trinity, keep it holy: to sow
to reap, to taste the sour bread of winter.

You stretch your fingertips against fires
in the far hills. You can get there from here.
Take no hot tea, no ginger snaps – go cold
and hungry. This is how the land wants you.

Turn west at the empty grain bins, watch with the owl
for mice and rabbits. When you enter the waist-deep
snow call out as though you might be heard by someone,
as if the cold had not already entered your blood.

A slow return

The deer listen, wait for the river to open its long dark throat.
Their hooves crack the hollow ice, a south wind drinks.

A weight is taken into their lungs. Cottonwoods
burn gray under a half moon.

The deer bend low amid slick reeds.
Tendons tighten, a twitch beneath the skin.

Grass shifts on a patch of bare earth above the scent of water.

The deer lift their heads – *thirst*, a smell blown back
from unseen hills, blown down from stars. The deer listen

to the rush of water under ice. The river suspends
clarity, old memory returns, breath is thrown off. Light seeps

through the sweetgrass, through lichen. The river wanders
east and the deer do not cross, as they track toward morning.

Mountain rain

Rainstorms arrive from the west.
All summer on this mountain
he has waited for rain
with no shelter except his skin,
no walls but those he plants
against the wind. There are no ghosts
of labour here or on earth.

Below him on the burnt plain men in farm houses
are smothered by abandonment. They have left the open fields
for confession, speaking of betrayals too violent for prayer.
Every reed, every blade
is blackened by drought.
In its shrunken form the mountain retreats into glory.

It is the moment before storm.
He sees it moving fast over the plains.
People move out of their farmhouses
and look to the sky as if to witness the art of angels.
Their minds crack open on verbs, though the minds of the people
mean nothing to the rain and the rain passes like a wave
over their heads, the cloud dreaming itself somewhere between
a flood and its own kind of wisdom, telling them:
forget many things,
lose many things,
forgive many things,
cast away many things.

Above the mountain lightning cracks open the sky,
kettle drum thunder, thrum of heart and rain enough to blind.
He turns his eyes upward, sees the roiling belly of the black cloud
as rain falls on the mountain and he sucks at it, he slurps it
he swallows,

knowing there are no words
for this thirst.
He no longer feels the cold rain,
           all he feels is cold.

Study the earth after the rain
and know the terror of angels and men.
Look outside the world
to the vanishing point.
The land has come to water
and it is not enough. Here rainwater
is a diversion flowing down the mountain,
ever downward. Rain is given to the dry earth,
histories of loss trickle into gossip
and man returns to light, and the rain whatever it dreams,
fill, pour, mouth full of prayer,
ventures onward above the earth
the way a river gives birth to the sky.

Mountain descent

Deer die in the low places, and sink into beauty. The man rests
at the peak of Last Mountain where the air smells of friction.
He looks out over the crust of the prairie, soon the plow will be
broken and the plow will multiply, steel blades breaking earth
with unobstructed will. It's as if his pupils can't take it all in until
he is made hungry and sane by the descending sun. It's then that
he feels something, something like faith. He sees antlers among
the brush and remembers the dream, the one that changes him into
a stranger.

The man on Last Mountain smells carcasses burning but does not
think of death, does not give in to memory. He looks across the land
as if he might turn back the intentions of men, or enter the dream of
the sleeping snake, the one that dreams of flight, the wind carrying it
away, a shadow wavering on the land. The man sees movement on
the horizon watches figures leap from light to darkness.

The usefulness of this dreaming is not clear to him. He doesn't know
how climbing the hungry road to the peak changes him, or how this
seeing leads to graver questions. In the dark, before he descends,
a stranger inside his body. He senses a giving over to eyes that dream,
a tongue that sings. He does not know the land dreams him, gives him
a new grammar – eyes of a deer, a face of violent beauty.

Still Mountain

Rain eases at the window and still men dig.
The deep water runs silent as a hunter.

Douse chickens with pepper, black flecks on feathers.
Each night in the woods coyotes sneeze.

Sleep without dream – a kind of blindness?
In the memory, a winter jack rabbit, black star hidden.

He turned his gaze to the sun,
a deer's heart upon his cutting board.

The fierceness slowly drained from my father –
window chair, and tyranny's long rest.

Cold accumulates – a painless ache.
Life flows backwards, for the man who lies down in snow.

In this country, comfort is to be forgotten,
we belong to winter, to its white amnesia.

Chimney smoke rises, an arrow, thin as first freeze.
Halfway up Last Mountain, he meets himself descending.

A pen skips, words speckle the page,
a parable for the eyes of the dead.

I want to spend my days looking at trees,
to be astounded each winter by their bright blankness.

Spring nods first to Last Mountain.
Do we have hope for a man in exile: warmth at last?

A certain kind of snow falls – round, polished seeds.
Our tongues reach for the very taste of memory.

The birds return to the mountain, small songs in the morning.
To them we are like ghosts departing, always departing.

I crouch in the reeds of the Qu'Appelle River.
Its sluggish current is neither for or against intuition

Twin boys are born: one blind, one with perfect sight.
Which will suffer the most?

Toleration – when I wanted another kind of paradox.
How far I have traveled from my own amazement?

To live on a mountain that is not mountain, is to scoff at God.
A three-legged dog loves the dark edges of his grave.

I sleep the sleep of the homesick; my heart awake.
There is a music that heals, but it is not in the poem.

I use the word *mountain* loosely, think of Christ with a lasso.
Adrenaline backed up in his body until he lit up the sky.

A man trades his black lungs for a pig's – every breath a soft squeal.
She dreamt the undertaker found deep in his throat: a crow's wing.

There is comfort in sorrow. To weep is also to praise.
In summer his daughters sang of his conceit – the song of his love.

Turning Mountain

1.

I seek Last Mountain
because it does not exist.

Approach it
from each direction
but you will fail to see it.

South: slip past it in the rain
though no rain falls on the mountain.
North: the heat fools you
your eyes turned by a blue heron.
East: at dawn you see hills rising,
as if to suggest that mountains will follow.
By noon the land of edges is lost.
West: ask a man in the mountain's shadow, where?
It's all around us, he'll say. *With us always, a blindness
a death, which does not exist.*

2.

First mountain or last mountain
it doesn't turn up on any road map.
Go back to the old ones,
overlay a grid road map,
and mark the mountain with a red X.

Travel again to the shadow
on paper. Travel toward an elegy
for the absent place.

Extend the lines of your X
obliterate towns, cities without regret.

The mountain monk advises,
Deny the real as well as the false.
Then he says,
I have no tongue to lie.

3.

The whole prairie
swells like an ocean.

The storm, magpie wing over the land
circles the red X, sends down fork
                        lightning.

Last Mountain island
sinks
beneath the darkening wave
that has no path.

4.

Here, where there was mountain
there is now empty space, ante-mountain.
Grid roads end here
fall off. Gravel floats up
forming constellations for the sun.

Finally, a brilliant sepulchre
of possibility. I enter
and with a small voice
make the horizontal vertical.

I open my ears and thunder
drops with the weight of mountain
turned in the hand of a god.

Leave things as they are.
You have already created the world.

5.

In the vast forests of the prairie great bears
once walked like kings. They wore purple cloth
for the sleeping eye of winter. The prairie whale
no longer climbs the sky with jade-green wings.
She sleeps below a disappearing cartography.
Gone are those names that blistered the tongue,
gone is our way of listening to the whispered
mutterings, the gurgles of the animals.
How well we have learned to listen through blood,
as trail fixes map to our bones.

6.

Step out
from the shadow of the mountain
which does not exist,
from the shade of trembling aspen.
step out from the grief depth of ash grove.
From the wary pines
carve a chair.

Stain the chair with the blood
of a deer. Paint the chair
with the wing of a magpie. His black,
his white are a perfect mask.

The chair is beautiful and useless
a cathedral in the wilderness.
Put the chair in a clearing
on the mountain.
Sit with the mountain,
sit down in the chair.

Let the mountain be more silent than the deer.
Let the mountain be slyer than the magpie.
Let it be truer than the prairie whale.

Let the mountain speak
from the bottom of the unknowing mind.
Let it speak with the tongue of necessity,
from the countenance of death, let it speak
of the forgotten paths of kingly bears.

Leaving this world

All day I have searched
these parched hills for a stone.
It is large and heaped with light.
I found it long ago but I was not ready
for that knowing, the red granite cradling,
sunlight and my back slick
my bones somehow comforted
by the rock bowl.

I catch myself asking for rain as I walk
as if I could pull it from the horizon by repeating
some long forgotten rubric,
rain pooled on the stones,
small mirrors for the sky.

A rough-legged hawk catches an updraft.
He sees all stones, carries their heat
into the sky. The hawk knows
all the ways to vanish.
Everywhere the grass is bent,
every living thing gives way to the wind.

I have sought anchorage
for too long. I have walked here
waited here, wanted to be the great stone,
to rise into the light
from a baptism of earth.

I cannot find the stone of my youth,
so I stand here with a useless memory
of rain. Enough,
God, make this enough.

Let it fill the stone bowl.
Let it wash the body.
Let us all cradle the rain.

It is what we leave,
it is what we are left.

Acknowledgements

Some of these poems have been published in *Grain, Wascana Review, Blue Jay, The Society, Regina's Secret Spaces: Love and Lore and Local Geography,* and CBC Radio's *Gallery.* Several of these poems appeared in the chapbook *When Seeing Fails* published by JackPine Press (December, 2006), and co-created with designer Tania Wolk.

The author is grateful to those who read these poems and gave invaluable insights and comments: The Poets Combine: Byrna Barclay, Robert Currie, Gary Hyland, Judith Krause, and Bruce Rice, and editors Eric Folsom, and Maria Jacobs. Special thanks to Allan Safarik who believed so strongly in this collection and who helped to shape it. Thanks also for the support and encouragement provided by Noelle and Simone at Wolsak & Wynn.

The author is grateful to Dorothy Knowles and the Mackenzie Art Gallery for providing the permissions to use "Dense Woods" on the cover.

Also thanks to Elizabeth George, Sharon & Peter Butala, Ken Wilson, Terry Fenton, Helen Marzolf, Tim Lilburn, Gary Seib, Donna Kane, Barbara Klar, Dave Sealy, Eric Greenway, Donald Ward, Emily Wilson-George and Sarah Wilson-George.

The irises is for Elizabeth George.
All Souls' & *The crows* are dedicated to the memory of Anne Szumigalski.
The Empress & the peonies is for Eric Greenway.
Words fall is for Patrick Lane.
Still Mountain is for Lorna Crozier.
Notes for touring the Museum of Winter is for Cam Forbes